SKALDIC VERSIFYING AND SOCIAL DISCRIMINATION IN MEDIEVAL ICELAND

By
GUÐRÚN NORDAL

READER IN ICELANDIC LITERATURE
IN THE UNIVERSITY OF ICELAND, REYKJAVÍK

*The Dorothea Coke Memorial Lecture
in Northern Studies
delivered at University College London
15 March 2001*

PUBLISHED FOR THE COLLEGE BY THE
VIKING SOCIETY FOR NORTHERN RESEARCH
LONDON

© UNIVERSITY COLLEGE LONDON 2003

ISBN: 0 903521 58 X

PRINTED BY SHORT RUN PRESS LIMITED EXETER

SKALDIC VERSIFYING AND SOCIAL DISCRIMINATION IN MEDIEVAL ICELAND

1

SKALDIC VERSIFYING WAS PRACTISED IN ICELAND FOR MORE THAN five centuries. It was one of the art forms which the settlers brought with them when they made their home in this remote island in the ninth century, and it did not give way to new poetic trends until the fourteenth century. We know frustratingly little of the way skaldic verse was communicated or understood in an oral, pagan culture, but the earliest written sources give us insight into the subsequent development of skaldic poetry in Christian society – particularly after 1100 – where it maintained its appeal to a particular section of society, the aristocratic, learned and religious community. The apparent continuity and consistency in skaldic versifying belies the radical social and cultural changes that took place over a five-hundred year period; changes that in themselves might seem to undermine the very foundations of skaldic verse-making and weaken its attraction and function in society. But not so. The strong and elevated position of skaldic verse in a Christian culture comes as a surprise, and we need to ask *why* verse firmly rooted in pagan myth held its own in the face of Christian Latin learning, even becoming the preferred medium for deeply religious poetry in the twelfth century, and *how* it redefined its role in the new Christianized culture. The answers to both these questions lie partly, I believe, in the relationship between formal school learning and skaldic verse in Iceland.[1]

The advent of literacy as a result of the Conversion of Iceland some thousand years ago serves as the dividing line between verse

---

[1] See a more detailed discussion in my book *Tools of Literacy. The Role of Skaldic Verse in Icelandic Textual Culture of the 12th and 13th Centuries*. Toronto, Buffalo, London 2001.

composed in a predominantly oral society on the one hand and in a written culture on the other. It is convenient to draw this line around 1100 when writing began and the new Christian culture had gained considerable ground. It was crucial for the development of the young written culture that the learned community, apparently beginning with Ari *fróði* ('the Learned') Þorgilsson (1068–1148), chose to write their historical works and learned treatises in the vernacular. Preference for the Icelandic language in historical writing – instead of Latin – could not however be guaranteed unless it was supported by a forceful and comprehensive educational policy in the cultivation of new generations of writers and learned men. But how could this be achieved? I will argue that skaldic verse was discovered at this early date as a crucial mediator between the study of *grammatica* in the schools and the indigenous oral traditions, thus ensuring that skaldic verse remained strikingly fashionable and 'modern' – so to speak – in medieval Iceland.

2

The gradual adoption of skaldic verse in an educational framework by the twelfth- and thirteenth-century élite is best explained by following the life of a key figure in securing skaldic poetry a place within the schools. Moreover the pattern of his life reveals the social discrimination inherent in skaldic versifying and in the documentation of skaldic verse in the twelfth, thirteenth and fourteenth centuries. The man in question, Einarr Skúlason, was born in Iceland *c.* 1090, first mentioned as a priest in 1114 at the court of King Sigurðr, the traveller to Jerusalem.[2] It is of note that his priestly status is highlighted on his first appearance in the sources, indicating that he must have been ordained before travelling to Scandinavia. He is never mentioned as a participant in political affairs in Iceland but there is an important reference to him in Ari Þorgilsson's list of high-born priests in 1143,[3] which implies that he was in Iceland at least at this time, possibly living

---

[2] *Morkinskinna*. Ed. Finnur Jónsson (Samfund til udgivelse af gammel nordisk litteratur 53). Copenhagen 1932, 375. English translation by Theodor Andersson and Kari Ellen Gade published as volume 51 in the *Islandica* series, 2000.

[3] *Diplomatarium Islandicum* I. Ed. Jón Sigurðsson. Copenhagen 1857–76, 185–6.

on his family's estate at Borg in Mýrar. The chronological list of court poets, *Skáldatal*, notes twelve kings and earls in Denmark, Sweden and Norway for whom he composed verse.[4] He rose to the distinguished position of *stallari*, 'marshall', at King Eysteinn Haraldsson's court. In 1152 or '53, when he was around sixty, he composed the first known metrical *vita* of St. Óláfr, where he refers to recent miracles that had occurred in Constantinople only a few years prior to the poem's composition. He recited the poem at the shrine of St Óláfr in Nidaros cathedral in the presence of King Eysteinn, King Sigurðr and King Ingi, and the newly appointed archbishop. His professional career abroad therefore spans more than forty years. He is not mentioned in the sources after 1160.

Einarr Skúlason's is a remarkable life of exciting contrasts. He was evidently born of a distinguished family, possibly educated as a chieftain's son in the first cathedral school in Iceland, run by Bishop Ísleifr at Skálholt from 1056: 'when chieftains and good men realized that Ísleifr was much more effective than other clergymen available in the country, many gave him their sons to teach, and had them ordained.'[5] We can surmise that Einarr enjoyed at least the minimal education befitting priests, notwithstanding the rudimentary state of education in Iceland in his time. Even though our sources are silent as to the details of the education of students at the early schools in Iceland, they would certainly have studied *grammatica*. *Grammatica* was the most important discipline in the schools, and every student would study the classical textbooks – and probably also the native ones when they appeared – as part of his education.

Our earliest sources seem to suggest that the theoretical analysis of language and composition included in the study of *grammatica* was from the very first period applied to Icelandic vernacular literature and to this end skaldic poetry proved the only fitting

---

[4] King Sǫrkvir Kolsson of Sweden (no verse preserved), Earl Jón Sǫrkvisson (no verse preserved), King Sigurðr Jórsalafari, King Eysteinn Magnússson, King Haraldr gilli, King Magnús blindi (no verse preserved), King Ingi Haraldsson, King Sigurðr Haraldsson, King Eysteinn Haraldsson, Sveinn svíðandi (no verse preserved) and the Norwegian chiefs Gregoríus Dagsson (only in the *Skáldatal* preserved with *Snorra Edda* in *Codex Upsaliensis*, DG 11 4to) and Eindriði ungi (also in *Codex Upsaliensis*). See *Edda Snorra Sturlusonar*. Ed. Jón Sigurðsson. Hafniæ 1848–87, III, 270–86.

[5] *Íslendingabók*. Ed. Jakob Benediktsson (Íslenzk fornrit 1). Reykjavík 1968, 20.

genre. The mid-twelfth-century *First Grammatical Treatise* shows clear acquaintance with skaldic verse. But why did skaldic verse interest its learned Christian author? Classical pagan poets, such as Vergil, Horace and Ovid, were the great authorities in the Latin textual culture which served as the foundation for the emerging vernacular literary culture in Iceland in the eleventh century. Their example was scrutinized in the grammatical literature and, presumably, influenced the way learned men in Iceland in the eleventh and twelfth centuries came to regard and treat their own indigenous, pagan literary heritage. By the thirteenth century the skaldic poets had taken their place alongside the Latin *auctores* referred to in the study of *grammatica* in the European schools, because they fulfilled the same criteria: they observed stringent metrical rules in their verse and alluded to pagan myth and legend in their imagery and kennings. These two distinctive features made skaldic verse a fitting model for the writers of *grammatica* in their explication of orthography and phonology and in their elucidation of rhetorical devices. The early pagan poets of the North were thus acknowledged and respected by the Christian community for their poetic excellence, in the same way as were the pagan Latin poets, such as Vergil and Ovid, in a Latin culture. Reference to pagan imagery was thus legitimized at the heart of the Christian culture, as is manifested in twelfth-century Christian poetry such as Einarr Skúlason's influential poem *Geisli*.[6] But how representative are these two pioneers, the First Grammarian and Einarr Skúlason, of their time? Our twelfth-century sources are too scarce to allow us to determine whether their view of the pagan indigenous tradition was accepted by the *whole* learned community as early as the mid-twelfth century, particularly by the early, and not wholly consolidated, Icelandic Church. However, the maturity of these early endeavours cannot be ignored, and they developed from a painstaking consideration of fundamental issues relating to writing in the vernacular as well as from a confidence in the native tradition in the face of the strong current of Latin Christian learning.

---

[6] Even though direct references to the pagan gods grew fewer in the 11th and 12th centuries (see Bjarne Fidjestøl. 'Pagan beliefs and Christian impact: The contribution of scaldic studies.' In *Viking Revaluations. Viking Society Centenary Symposium*

Four Icelandic grammatical treatises are preserved from the middle ages and all of them in manuscripts of Snorri Sturluson's *Edda*, the thirteenth-century textbook of skaldic poetics.[7] One manuscript from the fourteenth century, the *Codex Wormianus*, preserves all four together, and they are usually referred to by the order they are entered in that vellum, *First*, *Second*, *Third* and *Fourth*, which also accords with their likely relative ages. All four depend on or refer to skaldic verse. The first two treatises deal with Icelandic orthography and phonology, and both allude to skaldic verse in their treatment of the language. The First Grammarian writing in the middle of the twelfth century cites skaldic verse on two occasions, and he uses minimal pairs to distinguish between sounds and to argue for his spelling system. Minimal pair distinction is at the centre of his terminology, and is likely to have arisen, as Roberta Frank has pointed out, 'naturally in a cultural milieu trained to distinguish the alternating *skothending* and *aðalhending* of the skalds'.[8] The second is preserved in one manuscript in conjunction with Snorri Sturluson's *clavis metrica*, *Háttatal*, and sheds theoretical light on sound distinctions in the different types of skaldic metres. The third was written by Snorri Sturluson's nephew, Óláfr Þórðarson, in the middle of the thirteenth century, and contains both an account of orthography and phonology based on Priscian's *Institutiones*, and an analysis of the normative rules of style from Book 3 of Donatus's *Ars maior*. The *Fourth Grammatical Treatise* is the latest, written in the fourteenth century. It is an adaptation of Alexander de Villa Dei's *Doctrinale* and Eberhard of Bethune's *Græcismus*.[9] The third and fourth treatises, which are adaptations of classical textbooks in *grammatica*, cite a great number of skaldic verses by pre-Christian as well as contemporary poets, instead of translating the examples of the Latin original.

14–15 May 1992. Ed. A. Faulkes and R. Perkins. London 1993, 100–120), the pertinence of the pagan belief system to kenning constructions is never challenged by the poets.

[7] A fragment of a 'fifth' treatise is preserved in the A-manuscript of *Snorra Edda*, AM 748 Ib 4to.

[8] Roberta Frank. *Old Norse Court Poetry: The* Dróttkvætt *Stanza* (Islandica 42). Ithaca and London 1978, 37.

[9] Björn M. Ólsen. 'Indledning.' In *Den tredje og fjærde grammatiske afhandling i Snorres Edda tilligemed de grammatiske afhandlingers prolog og to andre tillæg* (Samfund til udgivelse af gammel nordisk litteratur 12). Copenhagen 1884, XLII–XLIII.

Learning was the privilege chiefly of men of Einarr's social class, men who belonged to the affluent and powerful section of society. The ease with which skaldic verse was adopted by the Christian community at large suggests a well-defined study of the medium in an educational context, inside and outside the Church, possibly by the twelfth century. The study of the art of skaldic poetry was in essence a study of skaldic versifying.[10] However, the poverty of documentation from the twelfth century should caution us against asserting that every learned establishment in the country followed the same educational policy, particularly the Church establishments. But even if this conjecture were judged tenable, it would not rule out the continuation of skaldic verse-making outside the school milieu and among the illiterate in society. It would however explain how skaldic verse became a crucial tool in scholastic learning and historiography in the late twelfth and thirteenth centuries. The successful introduction of the oral, pagan heritage in Latin Christian culture in Iceland through the intermediary characteristics of skaldic verse is – I believe – at the root of the flourishing literary production of the thirteenth century. There is an unequivocal tie between the art of the skaldic poet and the vernacular prose writings of the thirteenth century, as becomes apparent when we study Einarr Skúlason's work.

3

Einarr stands on the threshold of a new, exciting era when he starts school in the first years of the twelfth century. Even though there are no direct references to his school days, his metrical compositions bear witness to his learning. It would seem that his own verse-making was nurtured by academic training and that he composed verse which could be studied in a school framework. His impeccable command of internal rhyme and thus of the vowel system

---

[10] See Rita Copeland. *Rhetoric, Hermeneutics, and Translation in the Middle Ages: Academic Traditions and Vernacular Texts*. Cambridge 1991, 161, where she suggests that the works on poetics 'teach the art of composition through the art of formal literary analysis'. See also Douglas Kelly. 'The scope of the treatment of composition in the twelfth- and thirteenth-century arts of poetry'. *Speculum* 41, 1966, 261–78.

may suggest formal schooling.[11] Such stringent regularity is also attested by the poem *Háttalykill*, a *clavis metrica*, by the Orcadian earl Rǫgnvaldr kali and the Icelander Hallr Þórarinsson, composed at about the same time as Einarr's *Geisli*. *Háttalykill* apparently reflects a need for the systematization of skaldic metrics, and is at the same time rooted in royal chronology. The same intrinsic relationship between a study of skaldic versifying and royal *historia* is present in *Geisli*, as I will discuss later. Anne Holtsmark detected traces of Latin learning in *Háttalykill*, and suggested that it came into being as a verse game whereby two poets competed in composing a stanza in the same metre.[12] The rhyme is indeed very regular in these two twelfth-century poems, which may suggest a systematic study of language such as would be entailed in the study of *grammatica*. Regularity of rhyme alone cannot, however, determine the poet's learning. More significantly, we find in Einarr's corpus traces of instructional verse only preserved in the context of textbooks of skaldic poetics or in the grammatical treatises.

Few words need to be said about the provenance of the eleven verses by Einarr Skúlason which Finnur Jónsson arranged under the invented name '*Øxarflokkr*' – a poem about an axe.[13] This title is purely fictional, as is the existence of such a poem. However, some of these verses are clustered together in *Skáldskaparmál* in *Snorra Edda* in a way which indicates that they may have belonged together at an earlier stage. In *Skáldskaparmál* Snorri Sturluson rarely cites a sequence of stanzas by the same poet, and when he does the verses are most often drawn from the same poem.[14] We can

---

[11] See Finnur Jónsson's remark in his *Litteraturhistorie* II. Copenhagen 1923, 71–2 (2nd edition).

[12] In *Háttalykill enn forni* (Bibliotheca Arnamagnæanæ A1). Ed. Jón Helgason and Anne Holtsmark. Copenhagen 1941, 118–34.

[13] Jón Sigurðsson created the title '*Øxarflokkr*' (*Edda Snorra Sturlusonar*. Ed. Jón Sigurðsson. Hafniæ 1848–87, III, 364–5). The title has since been used for the verses printed together in Finnur Jónsson's *Den norsk-islandske Skjaldedigtning*. København 1912–15, A I 477–9, B1 449–51.

[14] This point needs to be discussed more fully in another paper, but I will note a few examples of this practice from the first part of *Skáldskaparmál*. The verse numbers are drawn from *Skáldskaparmál* 1. Ed. Anthony Faulkes. London 1997: 15–16 (*Sonatorrek*), 27–8 (*Vellekla*), 34–5 (*Vellekla*), 45–7 (poem by Eysteinn Valdason), 51–2 (by Bragi, 51 from *Ragnarsdrápa*, the other stanza is from an

therefore conjecture that the seven stanzas cited in the gold section (vv. 145–9, 193–4) originally belonged to the same poem, and probably the eighth cited separately in that same section (183). Another peculiarity in the case of some of these verses is the citation of whole stanzas, whereas Snorri's general practice in *Skáldskaparmál* is to refer to couplets or *helmingar*.[15] If we regard these eight stanzas cited in the context of gold-kennings as belonging to the same poem, it is striking that the imagery is only drawn from the myths of Freyja and Fróði. Einarr describes gold solely by reference to these two myths. The first five verses are cited in conjunction with Freyja and contain an energetic and accomplished elaboration on the theme of Freyja's tears, worthy of the brilliance we are familiar with in the author of *Geisli*. He shows his skill and knowledge of pagan myth by alluding to Freyja through her different family and social positions. In one stanza he describes the weapon through a reference to Freyja's daughter (*mær Gefnar*) *Hnoss*, whose name means a treasure. *Hnoss* is brought to the poet's bed (*beð*), as if the poet has received a woman from the king, not a weapon. The reference is not, however, improper, for the wording *leiða* 'lead' invokes the marriage ceremony. Citing the text of *Codex Regius*:

Ríkr leiddi mey mækis	The powerful controller of sword-meetings
mótvaldr á beð skaldi	[battles] led Gefn's [Freyja's] maid to the
Gefnar glóðum drifna	poet's [my] bed covered with Gautrekr's
Gautreks svana brautar.[16]	swans' [ships'] road's [sea's] embers [fire, gold].

It is noteworthy that Einarr Skúlason, the priest, describes the weapon in terms of pagan mythology, thereby linking his verses generically to earlier mythological poems in the context of gold-kennings such as *Haustlǫng* and *Ragnarsdrápa*, and producing an inventive and imaginative amalgamation of old and new poetic

---

unknown poem), 55–6 (*Húsdrápa*), 105–6 (by Arnórr, possibly from *Þorfinnsdrápa*), 113–14 (by Arnórr, 113 from an otherwise unknown poem, 114 from *Rǫgnvaldsdrápa*), 118–19 (from Hallfreðr's *Hákonardrápa*), 128–32 (by Einarr Skúlason).

[15] It is impossible to say whether the three additional fragments cited by Finnur in *Øxarflokkr*, two half stanzas (244–5) cited in sequence in the context of weapon kennings or the anonymous stanza from the *Third Grammatical Treatise*, belonged to the same poem.

[16] *Skáldskaparmál*. Ed. Anthony Faulkes. London 1997, v. 149.

traditions. In doing so, Einarr also endorses the instructional value of mythological poems composed in pagan times, such as *Haustlǫng* and *Þórsdrápa*, for generations of poets. It is striking that these poems, whatever their original context may have been, are only preserved in *Skáldskaparmál* in *Snorra Edda* and therefore only function in an educational framework. Einarr's intention in composing his stanzas is likewise descriptive and they too are only preserved in *Skáldskaparmál*, a work which typifies the didactic importance of skaldic verse.

4

Einarr Skúlason sought both to achieve social recognition at the courts of Scandinavian dignitaries, *and* to enjoy a privileged position in Iceland as a chieftain-priest, and he seems to have managed both. We could perhaps tentatively refer to his third latent occupation in life as skaldic scholarship. His verse-making also reflects two distinct but not exclusive subject matters, panegyrics of royal patrons and a celebration of the spiritual life of St Óláfr in *Geisli*, along with his instructional verse. These spheres are not contradictory, but complement each other, as is attested by the works of a number of poets in the twelfth and thirteenth centuries. Einarr Skúlason is perhaps not a typical man of his age, when we consider the 50,000 people living in Iceland in the twelfth century; his privileged background and opportunities in life immediately distinguish him from most of his contemporaries. But he can be compared to other men of his social standing who dominate the Icelandic sources of the twelfth and thirteenth centuries.

Einarr not only worked as a professional poet at the courts of distinguished Scandinavian rulers, he contributed to the establishment of the master-poets – or *auctores* – within Icelandic royal historiography. In doing so he sets an important example followed by Snorri Sturluson and other saga-writers of the thirteenth century. His poem *Geisli* is a pioneering work in many ways. Einarr is the first known Icelandic author to be commissioned by the court to compose a life of a Norwegian king, in this case a metrical hagiography of St Óláfr. He uses not only contemporary sources on the king's holiness in the poem, emphasizing Óláfr's sainthood by listing miracles that were witnessed after his death, he probably also relies on a lost version of *Passio Olavi* from the middle of the twelfth century, which is preserved in an Old Norse reworking in the Norwegian book of homilies. His sophisticated method of composition at this early date is of great interest. He is working in the middle of the twelfth century as a learned and skilled author, using and judging the reliability of a wide selection of sources: a Latin text, stories of miracles and skaldic verse composed for Óláfr. Einarr's poem is in effect the first saga of St Óláfr in the vernacular, and the thread between his poem and Snorri's Separate Saga of St Óláfr is unbroken. Einarr does not give a detailed description of Óláfr's life in the poem, but cites instead two of Óláfr's court poets, Óttarr svarti and Sighvatr Þórðarson, as sources for the saint's life:

Sigvatr frák at segði	I have heard that Sighvatr told about the
sóknbráðs jǫfurs dáðir.	deeds of the aggressive king.
Spurt hefr ǫld at orti	People have learned that Óttarr com-
Óttarr of gram dróttar.	posed verse about the king of the court.
Þeir hafa þengils Mœra –	They who were called men's master
því's sýst – frama lýstan,	poets have described the glory of the
helgum lýtk, es hétu	king of the Mœrir – that is done – I bow
hǫfuðskald fira, jǫfri.[17]	to the holy king.

This stanza is of particular importance because it is later echoed in Snorri's short version of the Prologue to the Saga of St Óláfr, preserved in the Bergsbók manuscript, which is also one of the two manuscripts containing the poem *Geisli* (the other is *Flateyjarbók*). Possibly following Einarr, Snorri Sturluson in his Prologue refers only to these two poets, Sighvatr Þórðarson and Óttarr svarti, as the most reliable sources for the life of St Óláfr.

I suggested before that the use of skaldic verse in the teaching of *grammatica* was at the root of vernacular saga-writing in the twelfth and thirteenth centuries, and that *Geisli* documented its links to royal historiography. Writers and poets such as Einarr in *Geisli* refer to skaldic stanzas composed by eleventh-century poets as their sources in works about the first Christian kings, but the sources for the

---

[17] *Geisli* 12, after *Bergsbók* (Holm perg. 1 fol.). Ed. Gustaf Lindblad (Early Icelandic Manuscripts in Facsimile 5). Copenhagen 1963, fol. 117rb, 7–9. Normalized spelling.

lives of the early, pagan kings would have been composed in a predominantly illiterate society. How could this pagan and early Christian verse – this important historical source – be rendered in the Latin alphabet? We can envisage a need for exact rules of orthography and phonology to secure a faithful presentation of the verse. The *First Grammatical Treatise* written at about the same time as *Geisli* admirably fulfils this need, even though its author does not indicate that the *Treatise* was written for that reason. The use of skaldic verse in the context of the study of *grammatica* in the schools was a necessary prerequisite for early skaldic verse to be respected as a reliable source in the historical kings' sagas, even though this approach may seem anachronistic as far as the old verse is concerned. Snorri Sturluson was aware of this fundamental requirement. He states in the Prologue to the Separate Saga of St. Óláfr:

> Þau orð, er í kveðskap standa, eru in sǫmu sem í fyrstu váru, ef rétt er kveðit, þótt hverr maðr hafi síðan numit at ǫðrum, ok má því ekki breyta.[18]

> The words which stand in verse are the same as they were originally, if the verse is composed correctly, even though they have passed from man to man, and that cannot be altered.

And he repeats this notion in the Prologue to *Heimskringla*:

> En kvæðin þykkja mér sízt ór stað fœrð, ef þau eru rétt kveðin ok skynsamliga upp tekin.[19]

> And the poems seem to me least disturbed if their metre is correct and they are interpreted in a sensible way.

A reliable rendering of these oral compositions in the Latin alphabet was therefore fundamental to the acceptance of the verse in the kings' sagas, which would give the authors – the master-poets – credibility in the written culture.

Critical selection from the most respectable poets, distinguished as the master-poets (*hǫfuðskald*) is a strong feature of the textbooks in skaldic poetics and the grammatical treatises, as early indeed as in the *First Grammatical Treatise*, and the importance of the poets

---

[18] *Heimskringla* II. Ed. Bjarni Aðalbjarnarson (Íslenzk fornrit 27). Reykjavík 1945, 422.
[19] *Heimskringla* I. Ed. Bjarni Aðalbjarnarson (Íslenzk fornrit 26). Reykjavík 1941, 7.

– or *auctores* – to official historiography is born out by *Skáldatal*, the list of poets. This list is preserved in two versions in manuscripts of Snorri Sturluson's works, the Kringla manuscript of *Heimskringla* and the *Codex Upsaliensis* of *Snorra Edda*. Its place in these two manuscripts highlights the strong relationship between the study of skaldic poetics and royal saga-writing, which is also apparent in the two twelfth-century poems, *Geisli* and *Háttalykill*. *Skáldatal* is not only a catalogue of poets, but primarily a list of successive kings and earls in Scandinavia. The composition of the list belongs clearly to the writing of chronology and genealogy, and to the compiling of records of the past which formed the basis for historical writing in the twelfth and thirteenth centuries. The affiliation of the list to the writing of kings' sagas is borne out by the fact that, as far as we know, not all the kings and earls listed in *Skáldatal* had poems composed for them. Yet they earn their place in the catalogue. All the works I have mentioned – the two poems, the *First Grammatical Treatise*, and *Skáldatal* – are products of the same cultural milieu.

Einarr Skúlason emphasized the authority of two poets in his poetic life of St Óláfr, and his own importance among the skalds was highlighted by the writers that succeeded him. His verse enjoyed unusual popularity in medieval skaldic scholarship. We have already noted that *Skáldatal* chronicles his service to twelve Scandinavian dignitaries, and he is cited extensively in the sagas of the twelfth-century kings. He is the most popular poet in Snorri's *Skáldskaparmál* (following the *Codex Regius* version), and he is quoted extensively in the *Third* and *Fourth Grammatical Treatises*. The critical selection of pieces by the respectable skalds in the works of *grammatica* and the kings' sagas may also be counted a political act, controlled by the élite who wrote or commissioned the writing of manuscripts and the composition of poetry. Einarr Skúlason belonged to this privileged group, and the preservation of his verse in – or in the context of – the kings' sagas and in the learned treatises reflects his cultural and social background.

5

The history of Icelandic literature is traditionally supposed to start with Sæmundr the Learned Sigfússon (b. 1056) and Ari the Learned

Þorgilsson who wrote important historical works in the late eleventh and the first part of the twelfth century. Each had the cognomen *hinn fróði*, which indicates the respect for their learning and their authority in the written culture. None of Sæmundr's writings exist, but Ari's *Íslendingabók* and his contribution to the writing of *Landnámabók* (the Book of Settlements) attest to his learning and knowledge of classical historiography. While their groundbreaking achievements are well known, the role of the poets in the development of vernacular saga writing has been less remarked.[20]

Einarr Skúlason is a near-contemporary of these two pioneers, and I would argue that his metrical compositions were also influential in shaping the textual culture of the twelfth century. His works are – as we have seen – deeply rooted in scholastic tradition, in the study of *grammatica*, royal chronology and skaldic poetics. Einarr Skúlason should be acknowledged as one of the most influential twelfth-century figures in the transition between the pagan tradition of the early skalds, and the new era in the late twelfth century where skaldic verse was given an eminent place in the textual culture of the time. Einarr Skúlason's position in the skaldic hierarchy and in the textual culture supports this claim. We witness variations on Einarr's life in the lives of many privileged men of his time and in the next generations; educated and high-born men who composed panegyrics for kings and earls as well as religious verse. I could mention two examples in the thirteenth century: the scholar, court poet and sub-deacon Óláfr Þórðarson, Snorri's nephew, the author of the *Third Grammatical Treatise* and possible author of kings' sagas, and Gizurr Þorvaldsson, the court poet and sub-deacon who became the first earl of Iceland in 1258. There are more such men of note who exemplify the strong hold of the élite on learning and skaldic verse-composition in medieval Iceland, which made skaldic verse one of the class symbols of the thirteenth-century Icelandic aristocracy.

The existence of a systematic study of skaldic verse in the context of grammatical literature does not exclude the active study of the

---

[20] I discuss this matter more fully in my essay 'Samhengið í íslenskum fornbókmenntum.' In *Sagnaheimur. Studies in Honour of Hermann Pálsson on his 80th Birthday, 26th May 2001*. Ed. Ásdís Egilsdóttir and Rudolf Simek. Wien 2001, 91–106.

art-form outside the schoolroom. It is likely that poets continued to learn their art in the same way as had been the practice of their illiterate colleagues of the past. We cannot exclude the possibility that the unknown poets represent a group distinct from that comprising the more privileged skalds; a group filled with poets of lower-ranking families who sought to strengthen their position in society by mastering the favoured art-form of the aristocracy. Moreover we must acknowledge that access to learning does not necessarily imply that all members of the élite were educated, only that education was most readily available to those belonging to the privileged classes to the exclusion of the less privileged and the community at large. Some poets who belonged to the ruling class could even have studied skaldic verse-making outside the schoolroom. Twelfth- and thirteenth-century sources rarely mention whether a person had enjoyed formal education; it is nevertheless possible to deduce from his activity in life and by scrutinizing his compositions whether he came from a learned background. Einarr's example is a case in point. The difficulty remains, however, that we have few means by which to ascertain the role which skaldic verse played in society generally, other than by analysing the historical sources, grammatical treatises and *Snorra Edda*. When we look closely at the profession of the twelfth- and thirteenth-century poet a picture of social discrimination emerges. But it only reflects the *tangible* evidence displayed by the manuscripts; that is, it reveals the élite's interests and their control of the information technology of the time: book production. Skaldic verse which did not meet its interests or which functioned outside their social milieu must regrettably remain hidden.

Skaldic and eddic poetry are the only known literary genres to have been transmitted from an oral culture and adapted to a written one, and the process of teasing out the service rendered by skaldic verse in the development of the textual culture in early Iceland brings to life the vigour and creativity of the literate community in the twelfth century. Today I have brought to your attention the intriguing implications of this phenomenon for Icelandic literary culture. The accomplishments of Einarr Skúlason and his contemporaries reveal the imagination and confidence with which these men embraced and overcame the cultural challenges of their time, and demonstrate how they redefined their heritage for the future.